Richard Meerlicht

Gedichte in der Krise

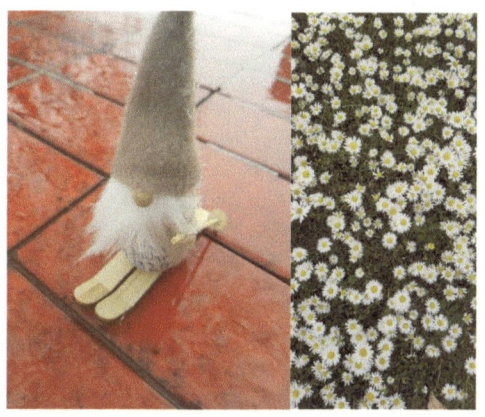

100 kleine Seelenwärmer in schwierigen Zeiten

Kontakt:
Richard.meerlicht@gmail.com

Herstellung und Verlag: BoD - Books on Demand,
Norderstedt
Dritte Auflage 2020, Originalausgabe

Printed in Germany

ISBN   9-783751-954792

**Bibliografische Information der Deutschen
Nationalbibliothek**
Die Deutsche Nationalbibliothek verzeichnet diese
Publikation in der Deutschen Nationalbibliografie;
detaillierte bibliografische Daten sind im Internet über
http://dnb.d-nb.de abrufbar.

Inhalt

Vorwort

Mitte März des Jahres 2020 fand ich mich im Brüsseler Stadtteil Ixelles plötzlich in einem Lockdown wieder. Der Frühling stand gleichzeitig vor der Tür und da man zeitweise nur noch um den Block spazieren durfte, kam mir die Idee, täglich ein kleines Gedicht zu schreiben, kombiniert mit einem Handyfoto der kleinen Spaziergänge oder einer Aufnahme vom Balkon aus. Diese Gedichte postete ich zusammen mit dem jeweiligen Foto täglich auf Facebook.

Im Laufe des Aprils entwickelte sich das Ziel, bis Mitte Mai 50 solcher kleinen Gedichte zu schreiben. Als absehbar war, dass dies gelingen würde, kam die Idee, diese Gedichte später in einem kleinen Bändchen zu veröffentlichen. Fünfzig Kurzgedichte würden jedoch selbst ein schmales Bändchen nicht füllen, deshalb wollte ich 50 zusätzliche Gedichte aufnehmen. Ich erweiterte deshalb die Sammlung im Laufe der Zeit nach hinten, in dem ich im Nachhinein für alle Tage bis Anfang März meist Vierzeiler hinzudichtete, kombiniert mit einem Foto aus dieser Zeit. Das ergänzte ich noch durch Bilder und Zeilen zu einer Reise Ende Februar/Anfang März nach Österreich und Ostfriesland sowie Elemente vom Jahreswechsel. Auch die unregelmäßig entstandenen Zeilen, die sich nach dem 16. Mai, dem Abschluss der intensiven Gedichtphase, ergaben, sowie Gedichte aus dem Jahr 2019, nahm ich in einem Nachspiel- und Rückschau-Kapitel auf. Mittlerweile ist bereits ein zweiter Band erschienen. Ich hoffe, es gibt Leser, die an diesen Vierzeilern, mehrheitlich auf Englisch geschrieben, Freude haben. Leider lässt eine preiswerte Publikation im Books on demand Verfahren mit aus Social media-Postings rückkopierten Bildern niedriger Pixelzahl keine hohe Druckqualität zu. Ich hoffe, die Leser sehen dies nach.

Wuppertal, im August 2020
Richard Meerlicht

1. Der Anfang

(Januar 2020)

Jahreswechsel 2020

The time gnome slides into 2020 in rain.
Even in the mountains hope for snow in vain.
What will the year bring to us?
What will be this year´s great big fuss?

(Picture: 11 likes)

Anfang Januar 2020

Der Reif die Pflanzen silbern macht
nach einer bitterkalten Nacht.
Die Wiese taut im Sonnenschein,
kann Winterlandschaft schöner sein?

(Bild: 10 gefällt mir)

7

2. Die Reise

(Ende Februar-Anfang März 2020)

28. Februar

Klagenfurt - so magisch in der Nacht,
wer hätte jemals das gedacht?
Lindwurm, Bachmann und Musil,
gibt´s ein besseres Kärnten-Ziel?

(Bild: 4 gefällt mir)

29. Februar

Im Februar konnte man noch lachen
und Café-Besuche machen,
Städte sehen
und dann suchen,
den allerallerbesten Kuchen.

(Bild: 2 gefällt mir)

1. März

Suurhusens Kirchturm so schief,
dass man gleich Guinness Books rief.
Jetzt gibt es einen Weltrekord
in diesem kleinen Friesenort.

(Bild: 2 gefällt mir, 1 Smiley, 1 wow)

2. März

Blauweiß der Himmel
und silbern der Sand.
Kleine Zauberinsel
im Friesenland.

(Bild: 8 gefällt mir, 2 wow)

3. März

Gebirge grauer Dünen,
Silberwelt des Sandes,
Melodie des Windes,
karge herbe Pflanzenwelt.
Die Seele spazieren führen
an der Gleichgültigkeit des Meeres.

(Bild: 2 gefällt mir)

4. März

Ein Schiff wird kommen,
und es bringt den Wunsch, den einen,
den man so wichtig nimmt wie keinen.
Ein Schiff wird gehen,
und es gibt kein Wiedersehen.

(Bild: 3 gefällt mir, 1 wow)

5 March

Groningen
The station´s historic passenger hall,
wonderfully old and very tall.
Interesting details rarely seen.
You miss something,
if here you haven´t been.

(Picture: 8 likes, 1 wow)

3. Der schwarze Schwan

(März 2020)

6 March

White swan in black night,
but soon a black swan at daylight.
An unexpected arrival,
soon all fighting for survival.

7 March

Arriving from a ride
at the stations bluish pride.
In an old steel town
of not that much renown.

(Picture: 6 likes)

8 March

On a narrow street,
strange things you meet.
A bookshop´s magic charm
making your soul so warm.

(Picture: 4 likes)

9 March

Working on statistics
The data´s clout,
how to figure it out.
Is counting beans
what it means?
See you later, indicator,
in a while, in a file.

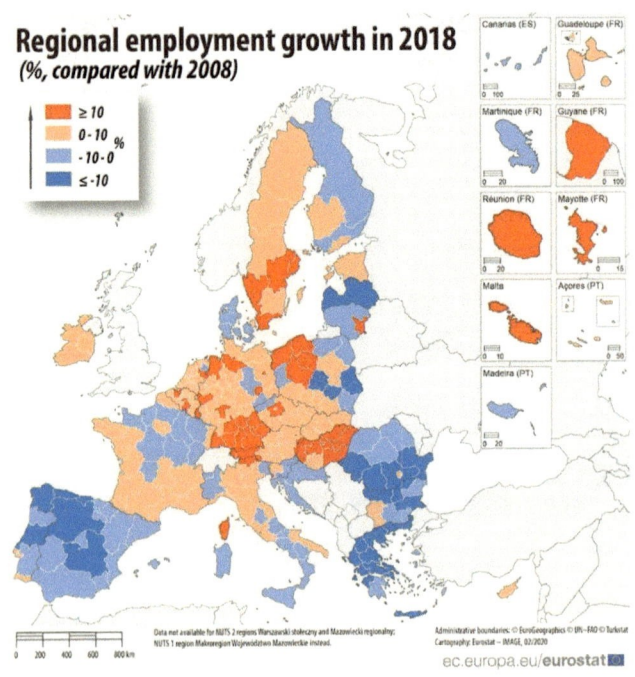

Regional employment growth in 2018
(%, compared with 2008)

≥ 10
0 - 10 %
-10 - 0
≤ -10

10 March

On this small lake
spring will awake,
after the winter´s freeze
with the willow trees.

(Picture: 4 likes)

11. März

Der Löwenzahn pustenbereit,
der Frühling ist schon ziemlich weit.
Der Lenz, er kommt sehr früh daher,
fast gibt es keinen Winter mehr.

(Bild: 1 gefällt mir)

12. März

Endlich etwas Sonnenschein,
für die Blumen ist das sehr sehr fein.
Gelbe Blüten gehen auf,
so nimmt der Frühling seinen Lauf.

(Bild: 5 gefällt mir)

13 March

Friday 13th, oh what a day.
Preparing for a lockdown
that somehow would stay.
Taking goodluckpills with
a four-leaf clover,
hoping the crisis will soon be over.

14. März

Die weiße Schlange kommt heran,
die weiße Schlange ist die Bahn.
Noch einmal eine Fahrt genossen,
denn bald wird alles zugeschlossen.

(Bild: 2 gefällt mir, 1 Träne)

14. März

Noch schnell nach Berlin,
noch einmal dorthin.
Danach wird´s ziemlich schwer.
Vielleicht geht´s gar nicht mehr.

(Bild: 4 gefällt mir)

15. März

In Zehlendorf auf dem Balkon
der Frühling kommt, man ahnt ihn schon.
Schon hell der Morgen-Sonnenstrahl,
die Bäume jedoch noch ziemlich kahl.

(Bild: 4 gefällt mir)

16. März

Was die Leute wirklich wollen,
es sind vom Klopapier die Rollen.
Als gäbe es kein morgen mehr,
kaufen sie alle Regale leer.

(Bild: 6 gefällt mir)

28

17. März

Meine Straße ist nicht ohne,
meine Straße ist `die Krone´.
Corona heißt´s auf Spanisch,
das Wort macht alle panisch.

(Bild: 5 gefällt mir, 2 Smileys)

18. März

Wer sich gesund ernährt,
der macht nichts verkehrt.
Nüsse und Beeren
Kannst immer verzehren.
Natürlich und frisch,
so soll´s auf den Tisch

(Bild: 6 gefällt mir, 2 Herzen)

30

19. März

Der Lenz, er kommt nicht angeritten,
der Frühling kommt mit leisen Schritten.
Kleine Bäume er in Blüten taucht,
die großen noch die Kälte schlaucht.

(Bild: 3 gefällt mir)

20. März

Ich hab ´ne Idee,
Zeilen ich seh.
Posting per day a line,
that should per se be fine.

21. März

Und bist du nicht billig,
so brauch ich Gehalt,
und ist´s Konto nicht willig,
so brauch ich es bald.

(Bild: 3 gefällt mir, 1 Smiley)

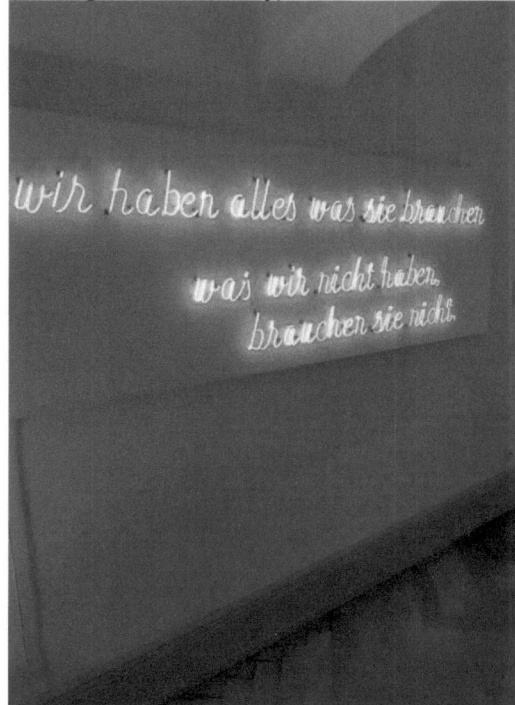

22 March

Every day this red box
with a postcard it rocks.
Throwing into the slit
a card with some wit.
Creating a smile,
at least for a while.

(Picture: 2 likes)

34

23. März

Der Frühling, der, er zögert noch.
Doch langsam, langsam kommt er doch.
Die Sonne hat schon viel mehr Kraft.
Der Winter wird bald abgeschafft.

(Bild: 8 gefällt mir)

24 March

An apple a day
keeps the doctor away.
But among the apples on top
is the modest Boskop.

(picture: 3 likes)

25 March

Times like this
and that is true,
break my heart
and make it blue.

(Bild: 6 likes)

26 March

A poem a day
keeps the sorrows away.
But bookshops are shut,
our supplies are cut.

27. März

Zeit für Veränderungen
Wer nicht ganz schlicht ist,
werde Schlichter,
wer nicht ganz dicht ist,
werde Dichter.

(6 gefällt mir, 1 Herz)

39

28. März

Im Jubelpark kein Jubel,
am Bogen auch kein Trubel.
Der Park ist ziemlich leer,
denn jetzt geht gar nichts mehr.

(2 geälfft mir, 2 zornig)

29 March

Another chilly day,
cold air not going away.
But blue sky and the sun
will soon give winter a run.

(4 likes)

41

30. März (Flashback 2013)

Ostern 2013 in Michelstadt,
wo es Schokoladenhasen hat.
Das ist hier halt so Osterbrauch,
ein Fachwerkrathaus, das gibt es auch.

30. März

Die Krise hat die Welt
vollkommen auf den Kopf gestellt.
2020, dieses Jahr,
wo nichts mehr ist,
so wie es war.

(2 likes)

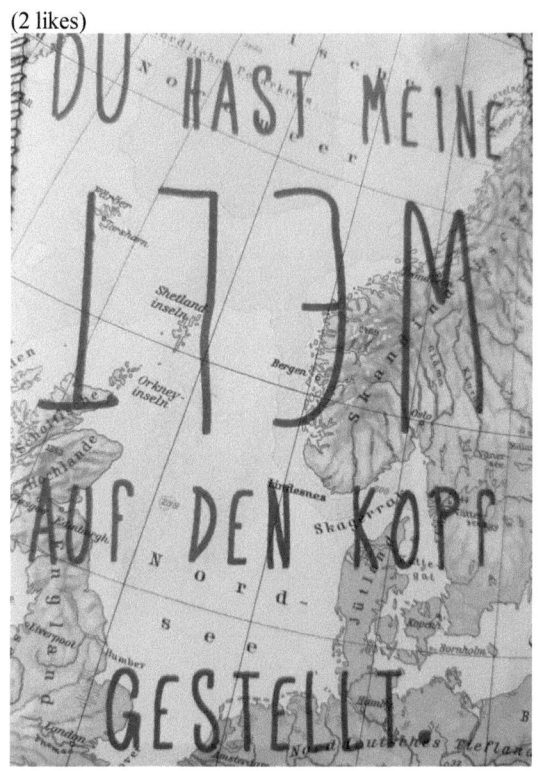

4. Gedichte im Lockdown

(Fünfzig Gedichte März-Mai 2020)

31. März

Tags die Sonne über Brüssel lacht,
nachts der Mond die Stadt bewacht.
Kalte Nordluft fließt herein,
es soll halt länger Winter sein.
Doch bald, bald kommt ein Frühlingshauch.
Warte nur, dann spürst du's auch.

1 April

Sun now finds its ways,
pushing away the cold days.
Spring is in store,
flowers galore.
Can you want more?

(1 like, 1 smiley)

2 April

Weather isn't good,
so not in the mood
to write a line.
I hope that is fine.

(8 likes, 1 heart)

3 April

One of its powers
lies in the flowers.
And more and more sun
provides also some fun.
The forthcoming spring,
that is the thing.

(5 likes, 1 smiley)

4 April

When nothing happens, what to write?
At least the days are now so bright
that temperatures turn into mellow,
which makes the bushes very yellow.

(6 likes)

5 April

You can always bet on
seeing a dandelion.
Even in streets with no name
it should be the same.
It's where I found
Taraxacum hanging around.

(1 like)

6 April

If you are going to Ixelles district,
be sure to wear some flowers on your car.
All across the nation,
such a springtime vibration.
But not so many in motion,
people with caution.

(5 likes, 1 heart)

7 April

Days now so bright
and flowers white.
And at the end of each tunnel,
there will be some light.

(5 likes)

8 April

Many leaves are green
and the sky is blue.
Tomorrow even greener,
I hope it will be true.

(7 likes)

9 April

Flowers abound
spring's around.
But to see Viola the flower,
you have to bend a bit lower.

(2 likes)

10 April

To find new flowers too lazy,
I come back to the good old daisy.
The daisies don't mind,
as long as I find,
their modesty not being crazy.

(8 likes)

11 April

On the street I see
more than one white blooming tree.
Despite spring being so nice,
before going out, let's better think twice.

(7 likes)

12 April

For every flower comes the day,
these already start to fade away.
Blossoms come and blossoms die,
as time goes by.
Reminding us that never
something lasts forever.
Still this makes our soul cry,
as time goes by.

(4 likes, 1 heart)

13 April

It's where Ixelles
really excels.
The large round pond
of which I 'm fond.
The trees around,
the spring I found.

(6 likes)

14 April

Despite many petals on the ground
blossoms still abound.
Why do you think
is the street so pink?
In times so bitter,
nature makes life sweeter.

(11 likes)

14 April (evening)

A bit of evening cycling around.
Here is what I found:
Brussels in silence,
but its heart still beats.

(7 likes)

15 April

It's not thistles.
It's the feathery bristles
carrying the dandelion seed
with quite some speed
to a better future,
at least, let's hope.

(2 likes)

16 April

Potentilla fruticosa
Little white flower
what's your name?
Is it important,
or just the same?
In the city you survive,
petals you have five.

(2 likes)

17 April

Ixelles has no mountain,
but a lake with a fountain.
XL, but tiny
and sometimes shiny.
Corners quite so-so,
but also lots of Art Nouveau.

(4 likes, 1 smiley)

18 April (morning)

Car redesigned by spring,
petals are the thing.
Petals small and white,
the car still looks all right.

(4 likes, 1 smiley)

18 April

On the sky more than a cloud,
but still a rose came out.
As time flows,
the flora grows.
Crisis lingers on and on,
but the day will come where it will be gone.

(3 likes, 2 hearts)

19 April

Brussels so green
as rarely seen,
and still some more
new leaves in store.
Emerald colours the city
with a palette so pretty.

(6 likes)

20 April

See what I found:
petals on the ground.
This is nature,
spring is mature.
Wind soon blows them away.
What is will never stay.

(6 likes)

21 April

We still have no Joyce.
Bookshops closed,
people with idleness overdosed.
But still hope for Ulysses' Bloomsday,
maybe in June, if not in May.

(2 likes)

22 April

In the block's shadow
a small flower meadow,
blooming yellow and white
on a day so bright.
Growing around a tree,
please come and see.

(2 likes)

23 April

A rose is a rose is a rose,
at least thus goes the prose.
But why so huge,
such sweet smelling deluge?
As if it wanted to say:
there will be no other day.

(7 likes, 1 heart)

23 April (evening)

Oh, have a look.
It's the day of the book.
Cervantes and Shakespeare,
each a great writer,
each made us brighter,
in 1616 left on this day,
but in our cultural memory
they will always stay.

(4 likes)

24 April

After the day of the Great Bard
a look at the backyard.
It's now so green,
it hasn't been
this year yet.
It won't get greener, I bet.

(2 likes)

25 April

Flagey at night
in peaceful light.
Around the pond a walk,
but nobody to talk.
Waterfowl around,
that' s all I found.

(7 likes)

26 April

Oh, this weather,
and even a feather.
A bird misses it, for sure it will,
but was it used as a poet's quill?
Life again plays the fiddle,
to give us another riddle.

(5 likes)

27 April

A house does hide
on the other side
of a square so round,
with a park so sound,
with plants so lush,
wanting a rain´s flush.

(4 likes)

28 April

It wasn't in vain
to hope for the rain.
It showered so loud
from many a cloud.
For a while it will stay,
driving sorrows away.

(4 likes, 2 hearts)

29 April

Innovation
Should we foster an innovation's early release
or is it the second mouse that gets the cheese?
Is it the early bird that catches the worm
or is the night owl patenting it the norm?
Do we really need unicorns
or better have cash cows with two horns?
Do we support agile gazelles
or better a university so that it excels?
Is it zombie or not to be
or should we have much more R&D?
Do dinos still have economic clout
or are they already schumpetering out?
Do not astound
that questions abound.

(1 wow)

30 April

Oh, this long straight track,
could it bring us back?
To the times, which were good,
times in a better mood.
From the moon to the sun
a place with more fun.

(3 likes)

1 May

Oh, these lazy days,
when spring the daisy lays
into the grass so green.
You know what I mean.

(1 like)

2 May

Nature still has in store
colours not seen before.
Almost a tower
of more than a flower.
Pinkish violet it be,
That is at least what I see.

(11 likes)

3 May

Destiny's funnel
got us into a tunnel.
It's dark inside,
but at the end some light.

(no likes)

4 May

Rain in May
and someone did spray
a poppy on the wall.
Nothing more, that' s all.

(4 likes)

5 May

As other flowers fade away,
a yellow one still has its day.
Exposing petal colours' might
to make the greyest day so bright.

(5 likes)

6 May

If you reach the gate and go beyond,
you find a waterlilies´ pond.
Plants in fifty shades of green,
at least, that's what I think I've seen.

(4 likes und 1 heart)

7 May

A sky so blue,
it is really true.
So green a tree,
all leaves you see.
What more to say,
the best month: May.

(5 likes)

8 May

What if you take
the path to the lake?
Is the water cold or mellow?
Is it deep or is it shallow?
The answer, my friend,
it lies behind the bend,
it lies behind the end.

(4 likes)

9 May

Single flower in white,
exposing its lonely pride.
Trying to attract a bee,
is this what here we see?

(4 likes)

10 May

Sunny Sunday, 10th of May.
Let's celebrate the Mother's Day.
In good times and in times of mess,
lucky who still a mother has.

(3 likes)

11 May

Mother's Day, plus one day more,
colourful flowers still galore,
despite an arctic cold air spell,
soon again all will be well.

(10 likes)

11 May (evening)

Oh sorry, one week late,
tribute to an Ixelles great.
Born in May 1929,
movie memories so fine.

(3 likes, 1 heart)

12 May

Time moves on,
but not always on a bed of flowers.
Sometimes in sunshine,
sometimes under rainy showers.

(3 likes)

13 May

Time's wheel,
the same old deal:
everything flows,
what's behind us grows.

(3 likes)

14 May

Lovely Auderghem
is still the same.
The green river's gentle flow,
plants around it still do grow.

(3 likes)

15 May

Never in vain
to look at the trees again.
All nature
now so mature.
All the leaves are out,
birds now chirp so loud.
Summer will come soon,
in less than one more moon.

(2 likes)

16 May

Poems - the end.
Fifty poems was not tough,
but fifty poems, that's enough.
Thanks to those, who read them all.
you helped to roll the lyrics ball.

(8 likes, 2 tears)

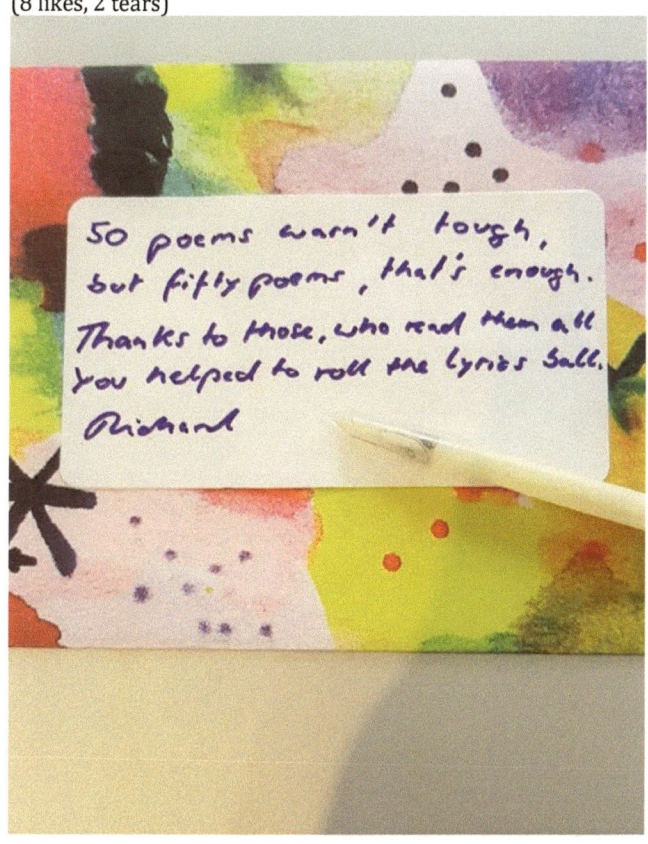

5. Nachspiel

(Zweite Maihälfte 2020)

17 May

In the middle of May
the first poem-free day.
Not spending time
with something to rhyme.
Nothing to post,
reading at most.

(2 likes)

18 May

Come what may,
what comes will stay.
The sun will sink,
the stars to blink.

22 May

The orange ones
they let me bet,
flower power,
not over yet.

(7 likes)

22 May

The ground is very stony,
this poppy is so lonely.
The soil is very dry,
the poppy wants to cry.

(6 likes)

26 May

Days now so long,
dusks so strong,
sky so clear,
summer is near.

(7 likes)

31 May

June knocking at the door,
but flowers still galore.
Marguerite´s milky way,
This galaxy could stay.

(9 likes)

6. Der Blick zurück

(2019)

April 2019

Almost heaven,
Western Allgäu.
White-blue mountains, Iller, Argen rivers.
Country roads, take me home
to the place, I belong.
Western Allgäu,
take me home, country roads.

(Bild 3 likes)

15. Mai 2019

Feeling blue in Bxl
Kein Bier auf Hawaii,
Weine nicht in Bordeaux,
Wasser auf der Ebene Müh(l)en.
Wie soll man sich denn fühlen?

(Bild 7 gefällt mir)

105

16 May 2019

Rain in May
moves all the troubles away.
Water falling from the sky,
feeling sad, I don´t know why.

17 May 2019

Every day passing this wall,
with the graffiti face so tall.
Who is this blue-eyed silver lady?
Who is this mask-guy so shady?

18 May 2019

ESC,
let's see
what this Saturday in spring
Song Contest drama will bring.
Outsider, or favourite's fall,
the winner takes it all.

19 May 2019

One of these empty days,
when the hair just greys.
Nothing happens at all,
only the rain does fall.

(2 likes)

20. Mai 2019

Es fährt ein Zug nach nirgendwo,
es fällt ein Blick nach irgendwo.
Die Scheibe gibt den Blick zurück,
die Scheibe, trennt sie uns vom Glück?

The end

(Fortsetzung folgt)

Blumen im Buch (Auswahl)

Deutsch	Englisch	Latein	Seiten
Löwenzahn	dandelion	Taraxacum	22, 50, 61
Frühlings Adonisröschen	adonis floret	Adonis vernalis	23
Forsythie	golden bells	Forsythia	49
Gänseblümchen	daisy	Bellis perennis	48, 55,69, 74, 79
Waldrebe	clematis	Clematis	57, 80
Kirschbaum	cherry tree	Prunus tomentosa	59,67,70
Strauchiges Fünffingerkraut	shrubby cinquefoil	Potentilla fruticosa	62
Rose	rose	Rosa	65, 70
Gerbera	gerbera	Gerbera	69, 83
Weiße Lichtnelke	white carnation	Silene Latifolia	87
Filziges Hornkraut	felt hornbill	Cerastium tomentosum	88
Ziertabak	ornamental tobacco	Nicotiana alata	89
Ringelblume	pot marigold	Calendula officinalis	99
Klatschmohn	poppy	Papaver rhoeas	100

Weitere Gedichtbände von Richard Meerlicht

Gedichte eines Sommers
100 kleine Lichtstrahlen in schwierigen Zeiten
(Juni-August 2020)
Books on Demand, Norderstedt, 2020